DREAMS&VISIONS

A Way into Prayer for Young People

Jill Fuller

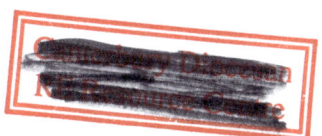

Illustrated by Mike Lacey

First published in 1997 by
KEVIN MAYHEW LTD
Rattlesden
Bury St Edmunds
Suffolk IP30 0SZ

0 1 2 3 4 5 6 7 8 9

ISBN 1 84003 075 5
Catalogue No 1500147

Cover illustration: Graham Johnstone
Cover design by Jaquetta Sergeant
Edited by David Gatward
Typesetting by Louise Hill
Printed and bound in Great Britain

CONTENTS

INTRODUCTION

This book is about your own spiritual quest. It is about developing your own inner life and resources, discovering your own feelings and exploring the patterns and attitudes which you are establishing in your life. It is also about examining the possibility and risks of travelling through your life in the company of the Spirit of God.

I wonder if you ever share a journey with a good friend? Justin and Kelly are friends who share journeys. They had known each other for some years as they had lived in the same street. When Justin moved to another part of the town they had kept in touch and although they now attended different schools they agreed to meet on the bus each day and chatted. It wasn't always easy to find a seat together away from the noise where they could speak privately but they managed most days and on Fridays they got off the bus and walked to a cafe in town where they could exchange their news. Sometimes they simply shared the everyday events, a video they had enjoyed, a joke they had heard, classroom gossip. But they also talked about more important issues. When Justin's mother left home, Kelly had listened to his grief and sadness and helped him when he had to make difficult decisions. When Kelly was being bullied at school it was the courage she received from Justin's friendship which helped her tackle the situation. Best of all was the trust between them. They knew that they could tell each other everything in confidence without fear of being ridiculed or misunderstood, but they also knew that they would challenge each other and would not always agree. Justin and Kelly were good friends who shared a journey.

I believe that prayer and spirituality is in some ways similar to the experience of both friendship and journeying. It involves an inner journey during which one explores and reflects on one's own life, personality and decisions. Prayer is also concerned with a desire to meet and have a friendship with God, a commitment to finding a time and a place, a willingness to listen as well as to speak and an openness to the stillness as well as the movement of God's Spirit.

A TIME AND A PLACE

Do you know this song which comes from *West Side Story*? It is sung by Maria and Toni:

There's a place for us,
Somewhere a place for us.
Peace and quiet and open air
wait for us somewhere.
There's a time for us,
someday a time for us.
Time together with time to spare,
time to learn, time to care.
Someday, somewhere.

The yearning of the lovers in *West Side Story* is similar to the yearning of those who seek God. But if we really want to make the meeting with God a reality, we have, as with all meetings with friends, to fix a time and a place and to view it with the same kind of commitment and urgency as we would give a promise to a friend. A good friend is understanding, will be ready to change the venue from time to time or wait for us if we are late. But if we repeatedly fail to turn up or make excuses the friendship becomes shallow and meaningless.

If this book is to be of any use to you, you will need to decide for yourself a time and a place each day which you can set aside to develop your friendship with God. This may not be easy. At first a period of about five to ten minutes is suggested but you may want to extend this as you progress. When is the best time for you? Immediately on return from school when you might combine the prayer exercises with having a cup of coffee? Or are you an early bird who enjoys being about in the quiet of the morning? The time you choose may also be determined by the availability of a quiet, uninterrupted space. You may be fortunate enough to have your own separate bedroom where you can be alone. If not, you may need to be resourceful in finding a time when a place in the house is not being used by others and this may need some negotiation. If space is not available at home you may find that there is a local church you could sit in, or maybe there is a room or library at school.

USING THIS BOOK

It may help to browse through this book before using it. Turn to the Contents page and read it through. You will see it is divided into seven Prayer Moods:

EXPLORING
THANKSGIVING
ATTENTIVE LISTENING
WONDER AND WORSHIP
INTERCEDING – THINKING OF OTHERS
TRUSTING
IMAGINATIVE CONTEMPLATION

As you read be aware of which 'mood' appeals to you most. The mood is meant to indicate the general atmosphere or feeling of the prayer.

Each Prayer Mood has four accompanying Focus pages. These pages contain ideas to help you develop the prayer mood. As you read these, be aware of which titles attract you most. Sometimes the ideas on the Focus page will need planning in advance. Occasionally they will need simple equipment such as paper or felt tips, and sometimes they require action such as a walk or watching the television. Plan in advance so that you do not have to interrupt your time of quiet to fetch a pen or find a book. The way you choose to use this book depends on you. You do not have to work through it from cover to cover but can dip into ideas as they appeal to you. However, do not rush or try several ideas in one session. If one particular Focus is helpful and productive for you, use it on several occasions. If the Focus does not appeal to you leave it out, but be prepared to look at it another time.

The time spent using the book is for your benefit and growth. Only you can tell what helps you most. It is your journey and your friendship with God.

JILL FULLER

ACKNOWLEDGEMENTS

The publishers would like to express their gratitude to the following for permission to include copyright material in this publication:

Campbell Connelly & Co Ltd, 8/9 Frith Street, London W1V 5TZ, for the text of the song *Somewhere* (Bernstein/Sondheim), © Copyright 1957 (renewed) Leonard Bernstein, Stephen Sondheim. Jalni Publications Inc., USA & Canadian publisher; G. Schirmer Inc., worldwide print rights and publisher rest of the world. International Copyright Secured. All Rights Reserved.

Mrs P. E. Dale for the translation of Matthew 25:31-46 by Alan T. Dale, taken from *New World*.

Kingsway's Thankyou Music, PO Box 75, Eastbourne, East Sussex, BN23 6NW, for the song text *From heaven you came, helpless babe (The Servant King)* by Graham Kendrick, © Copyright 1983 Kingsway's Thankyou Music.

The Merlin Press Ltd (Green Print), 2 Rendlesham Mews, Rendlesham, Woodbridge, Suffolk IP12 2SZ, for the two extracts by Milder Masheder from the publication *Let's Play Together*.

Penguin UK, 27 Wrights Lane, Kensington, London W8, for the short extract from *Ann Frank's Diary*.

Unless otherwise stated, Bible quotations are from the New Revised Standard Version, copyright 1989 by the Division of Christian Education of the National Council of Churches of Christ in the USA. Used by permission.

First Prayer Mood

EXPLORING

This prayer mood is to help you explore and reflect upon your personality and to consider the direction you want your life to go.

Christians believe that a loving God created the world and that each person is unique, of inestimable value and loved by God. This means that there has never before been anyone exactly like you and never will be again in the future. Your particular personality and gifts will never be duplicated. Prayer Focus 1, 'Who are you?' and Prayer Focus 4, 'When do you feel at home?' are designed to help you explore and reflect on your God-given personality.

Christians believe that Jesus was sent by God to show us the extent of God's love and to give us an example of a life committed to loving. The command of Jesus to his followers was to 'love one another as I have loved you' (John 15:12). It is the exploration of the meaning and significance of this commandment and its implications for the way we choose to live our lives which forms the springboard of Prayer Focus 2, 'What are you looking for?' and Prayer Focus 3, 'Where are you going?'

Who are you?

In magazines and newspapers there are often interviews with famous people. These articles are sometimes called 'profiles' and generally tell the reader about the person's background, likes and dislikes, achievements and disappointments, and their hopes and fears for the future.

Imagine that you have the opportunity to interview someone you admire or who interests you. Write down about ten questions you would like to ask him or her.

Now imagine that you are being interviewed. Ask yourself these questions and jot down the answers. Alternatively you may like to do this exercise with a trusted friend. Try to be as honest with yourself as you can – your answers won't be published! At the end look carefully through what you have written.

- Have you found out anything new about yourself?
- Did any of your answers surprise you?
- Are there talents you would like to develop?
- What are you going to do about that?
- Are there aspects of your way of life which you don't like?
- Can you talk to someone who could help you?
- Have you a dream for your life?
- What must you do to help this become a reality?

You may like to put these ideas or plans down and to look at them from time to time.

Concluding Reflection

Jesus came to tell the world
    that each person is precious in the sight
    of God.
Jesus came to help us
    to find fulfilment and purpose in life.
You are unique and precious.
Your life has a purpose.

I have written your name on the palms of
    my hands.
    (Isaiah 49:16)

Who are you?

On this page stick a photograph of yourself and write your profile.

_____

_____

_____

_____

_____

_____

_____

_____

_____

_____

_____

What are you looking for?

John the Baptist was standing with two of his disciples when Jesus walked by. John looked at Jesus as he passed and said, 'There is the Lamb of God'. When the disciples heard this they followed Jesus along the road. Jesus turned and saw them following and asked, 'What are you looking for?' (adapted from John 1:35-38)

What are you looking for in your life? What is important to you?

Imagine that you are very old and nearing the end of your life. As you lie peacefully in your bed you can hear people talking about you in the next room. Which of the following sentences would you like to think were true? Are there any you would rather not hear? Which is the most important to you? Which matters least to you?

• S/he was always such a loving and friendly person.

• S/he had lots of friends.

• S/he always seemed to be having fun.

• S/he made lots of money and was very wealthy.

• S/he always seemed contented.

• S/he was very successful in life.

• S/he achieved a position of great power at work.

• S/he loved her family.

• The family loved her.

• S/he owned an expensive car/house/ yacht/villa abroad.

• S/he did so much for others in her life.

Think about your answers. What do they tell you about what you are looking for in your life? What are your life values? How do those values affect the way you are choosing to live? You may like to write down what you are seeking.

Concluding Reflection

When he was on earth Jesus often challenged his listeners by asking them questions.

He asked the disciples of John, 'What are you seeking?'

In quietness ask yourself, 'What are *you* seeking?'

What are you looking for?

In the spaces below write what you would like to hear people say about your life.

Where are you going?

This is a story about a young man who had a dreadful experience on a journey, an experience which changed the direction of his life. We will call him Frank.

As a young man, Frank was taken prisoner during the war and along with other prisoners was being marched to a camp. It was bitterly cold with deep snow on the ground. The prisoners were cold, hungry and exhausted but the soldiers in charge of them allowed no rest, and continually bullied the sorry line of men, women and children to keep marching.

Amongst those walking near Frank was a young woman. She was heavily pregnant and had with her three small children. She carried the smallest, whilst the other two clung to her coat to keep themselves from falling in the snow. So it was that she trailed further and further behind the long file as they tramped onwards. The guards would not allow Frank or anyone else to help her; instead they shouted and hit her with their rifle butts, urging her to keep up with the rest. At last, exhausted, she collapsed in the snow. The guard turned round and without hesitation shot her dead. When the tiny children fell crying upon their mother he shot the children too.

Utterly sickened and distraught, Frank struggled onwards, but years later he was to tell how that moment changed his life for as he walked through the blizzard he asked himself many questions:

- What did the woman's life mean?
- Did human life have any sense or purpose?
- How could he come to terms with suffering and cruelty?

- Could he ever forgive the guard for his brutality?
- Could he ever forgive himself?
- How could he cope when apparently powerless in the face of injustice and inhumanity?
- What was the purpose of his future life?
- Was there any God who cared?
- Was there any way of living which could help him to make sense of his experiences?

Hopefully very few of us will ever personally experience such traumatic events as Frank, but television and radio reports leave us in no doubt that brutality, cruelty and pain exist. Hopefully many of us also experience love, friendship and a sense of community and can also see signs of compassion and heroic efforts to care for the world and its inhabitants.

What advice would you give to Frank as he considered his response to his experience?

Concluding Reflection

How will you live your life?
What is most important to you?
What is the purpose of your life journey?
How will you respond to pain, injustice, disappointment, success, failure, happiness, rejection?
What pattern has Jesus given us?

Where are you going?

In this space write a letter to Frank giving your response and reactions to his questions.

Prayer Focus 4

When do you feel at home?

Have you ever noticed how sometimes you may feel completely comfortable and peaceful, an experience which could be described as being 'at ease', or 'at home' with oneself. At other times you may feel restless, unsettled or miserable. We are each unique and need to discover which environment best helps us to 'feel ourselves' and also challenges us to explore areas where we might further develop our gifts.

You may like to do the following exercise alone, with a friend or in a group.

Look at the drawings opposite. Take time to imagine yourself into each situation. Ask yourself the following questions:

- Which situation do you feel most at ease in?

- Can you identify what it is you like and enjoy about it?

- Where would you feel most ill at ease? Can you explain why?

- Are there any of these situations you would prefer to avoid? Why?

- Would you like to explore those situations which at present you find difficult?

- Is there any way you could do that? How?

- Are there any discoveries you have made about yourself which you would not want to share? Can you explain why?

- What do your discoveries teach you about yourself and the choices you may want to take in your life?

When do you feel at home?

Second Prayer Mood

THANKSGIVING

Have you ever been in a situation when you have put yourself out to do something kind or helpful, and your effort has not been acknowledged and you received no thanks? If so, you will realise how important thankfulness is. Yet we ourselves often go through life missing the very obvious gifts and benefits which we receive each and every day and failing to rejoice and be thankful. How often do we take for granted our health, our food, our friends and indeed the very gift of life itself?

In the accounts we have of the last meal which Jesus shared with his disciples we are told Jesus 'took bread and when he had given thanks he broke it and gave it to them'. This attitude of thankfulness is important and indeed the central service of the Christian community when bread and wine are shared is sometimes given the name 'Eucharist' which means thanksgiving.

Paul wrote to the early church community in Ephesus urging them to give 'thanks to God the Father at all times and for everything in the name of our Lord Jesus Christ' (Ephesians 5:20). However, on many days we may feel ungrateful, miserable, rejected and totally lacking in the spirit of thankfulness. The exercises in this section are to help us to open our eyes once more to the world around us. They are designed to alert us both to the presence of the loving spirit of God and to our responsibility to respond in a spirit of loving care and thankfulness.

Prayer Focus 5, 'A prayer walk', encourages a reflective awareness of our surroundings. Prayer Focus 6 meditates on the gifts of our bodies. Prayer Focus 7 is an exercise to use at the end of each day whilst Prayer Focus 8 looks at relationships and community.

A prayer walk

Have you ever reached the end of a journey without noticing anything on the way, or how you got there? Perhaps your journeys to school are like that?

This next exercise is to help you to become more alert to the world around us and to appreciate with thanksgiving how all we see and hear can be a way of God speaking to us.

Plan and time the route of the walk beforehand or choose a route that is already familiar. It is important that the mind should not be distracted by anxieties about losing the way or not returning in time for supper! The length of the walk can vary according to the time available. You may like to walk with a friend or in a small group so that you can share thoughts afterwards. This would also enable one person to take responsibility for the route and timing. Try to be silent during the walk itself and allow time for sharing insights afterwards. Aim to use all your senses of observation: sight, touch, hearing, smell, and involve your mind and imagination.

SAFETY REMINDER

In planning this walk ensure that your route is safe. It is always important to walk in daylight and to let someone know where you are going and when you expect to be back.

During the walk be aware of everything you see, hear or observe. This could be:

- the distant view of hills
- the reflections in the windows of a tower block
- a bird building its nest
- the contents of a skip on a building site

Sounds could include:
- the transistor radio of some workmen
- the rushing of water over stones
- the shudder of a pneumatic drill
- the quiet munching of cows in a field

Allow time to appreciate textures too:
- the roughness of the bark of a tree
- the coldness of a metal handrail
- the smooth coat of a cat
- the sharpness of a pebble-dashed surface

Be observant of what is happening around you as you walk:
- a child walking with its parent
- a farmer working in the fields
- a derelict house
- someone sitting on a park bench

On your return you may like to discuss your observations and thoughts with your friend or write or draw them in the space opposite.

Concluding Reflection

Open my eyes that I may truly see,
open my ears that I may listen
with care,
refresh my resolve that I may walk
in the ways of your teaching.
Amen.

A prayer walk

In the space around this prayer draw or describe in a few words some of the things you have noticed on your walk.

May the spirit of thankfulness fill all my life.
May thanks touch the depths of my heart.
May the whole of my being resound with God's praise,
    reflecting God's love in each part.

May I notice God's love in the everyday things;
    give thanks for the daily routine.
May I recognise God in the eyes of my friends
    and the places to which I have been.

May I know that God's Spirit accompanies me
    on every step of the way.
Whatever the pleasure or worry or pain,
    God's Spirit is with me each day.

And so may I travel in peace and in joy,
    with thanks at the depth of my heart;
    for I know that a Love beyond all I dare hope
    redeems my whole life in each part.

Your amazing body

Until we are ill or have an accident we tend to take our bodies for granted, only noticing them when they are tired or painful. Take time to consider the everyday miracle of your body.

If you don't know much about how your body works, it would be worth while browsing through some books on the subject and becoming aware of how amazing it really is.

For instance, did you know that:

- You make 100 billion red blood cells every day
- When you touch something a message travels to your brain at 124 mph
- Your eyes can distinguish up to one million colour surfaces
- When you smile you exercise 30 muscles.

- You have copper, zinc, phosphorous and nickel in your body (among other things) and gold in your toenails
- The carbon in your body was made by dust flung out from the stars

Sit comfortably in a chair and allow time to become conscious of different parts of your body and how they function:

- Bones and muscles
- Brain and nervous system
- The five senses
- Heart and lungs
- Digestion
- Reproduction

Use the words on the Focus Page to help you think about these things.

Your amazing body

In a relaxed position concentrate your attention on the different aspects of your body:

Bones and muscles

Move your hand, fingers or toes and think of the processes involved in these seemingly simple actions. With an act of will you are able to control your physical movements quickly and accurately. Your bones are strong and hard and provide a firm framework for your body, but they are also relatively light, and the intricate way in which they are jointed and supplied with muscles and tendons enables them to be extraordinarily flexible.

Brain and nervous system

The very fact that you are thinking and feeling and are conscious of these thoughts and feelings is a mystery in itself. Nobody really knows what consciousness really is or how it works, but it seems to be centred in the brain which is a mass of ten billion neurones or nerve cells. The brain and nervous system have been compared with a telephone exchange, a computer network and a library, but they are far more complex than all of these put together.

The five senses

Sight, hearing, touch, taste and smell. Think of these in turn and ask yourself how they work. Light waves and the eye; sound waves and the ear; sensitive nerve cells in the skin which can distinguish different textures and temperatures; taste buds and olfactory glands by which you can tell sweet from sour, strawberries from coffee, wood smoke from newly mown grass. Think of how the nervous system carries these messages to your brain where you can experience them.

Heart and lungs

Be aware of your breathing and heart-beat. They are signs that your body is being continually supplied with fuel automatically, without you having to think about it at all. Your blood carries oxygen from the lungs to every cell in the body. It also transports digested food, hormones and waste products as well as fighting against disease and infection. It is truly called life blood, because your very life depends upon it.

Digestion

The way your digestive system is able to turn food into flesh and blood, bone and energy, without you having to do anything about it except eat and enjoy it, is yet another marvellous feature of the biological machine you call your body. When your mouth waters and your stomach rumbles you know the system's working.

Reproduction

Perhaps the most amazing gift of all is the ability to reproduce another human life, just as your parents produced you. But you must do it in co-operation with a partner of the opposite sex. You cannot do it alone. God has made your body in such a way as to encourage you to love.

The fruit of experience

Memories are very important to us as individuals, as members of a community and as a nation. This becomes more apparent when people suffer from memory loss or when memories of a nation are suppressed or distorted.

Sometimes, our brain needs reminders to 'Save and continue' and the habit of reviewing each day, and 'banking' our memories can help us to become more aware and thankful of what these everyday 'blessings' are to us. We can develop the habit of looking for the positive aspects of each day on which we can build as well as learning from experiences which may feel negative and painful.

At the end of each day before you go to sleep take time to reflect on the day you have just experienced. Remember this is a day of your life which will never be repeated. It may help you if you can sit in a comfortable chair or lie on your bed with your eyes closed. If possible find somewhere which is free from the noise of television or radio and where you won't be interrupted.

Try to recall the whole of the day beginning from when you awoke through to the present moment. Be aware of your feelings and emotions, times of exhilaration, success, disappointment, anxiety.

Try to 'bank' at least three good memories and to give thanks for the blessings of the day:

- a joke shared with a friend
- an exhilarating game
- an argument resolved
- a task achieved
- a good meal

Take time to think over any event, feeling, relationship or problem which is bothering you or making you feel anxious, angry or unhappy:

- Do you need to share this with someone? Who? When?
- Is there anything you need to do to put the problem right?
- Is there anything someone else could do? Can you ask them for help? When? How?
- Is there anything you could learn from an unpleasant experience of the day?
- Do you need to 'let go' of any memory, learning from it but refusing to let it spoil the next day?

On the Focus Page opposite draw or note something down about your experiences below the bulbs. Imagine these experiences growing and maturing into a positive aspect of strength and fruitfulness in your future. Write about these in the space above the flowers.

The fruit of experience

'The flowers of all our tomorrows are in the seeds of our todays.' (Source unknown.)

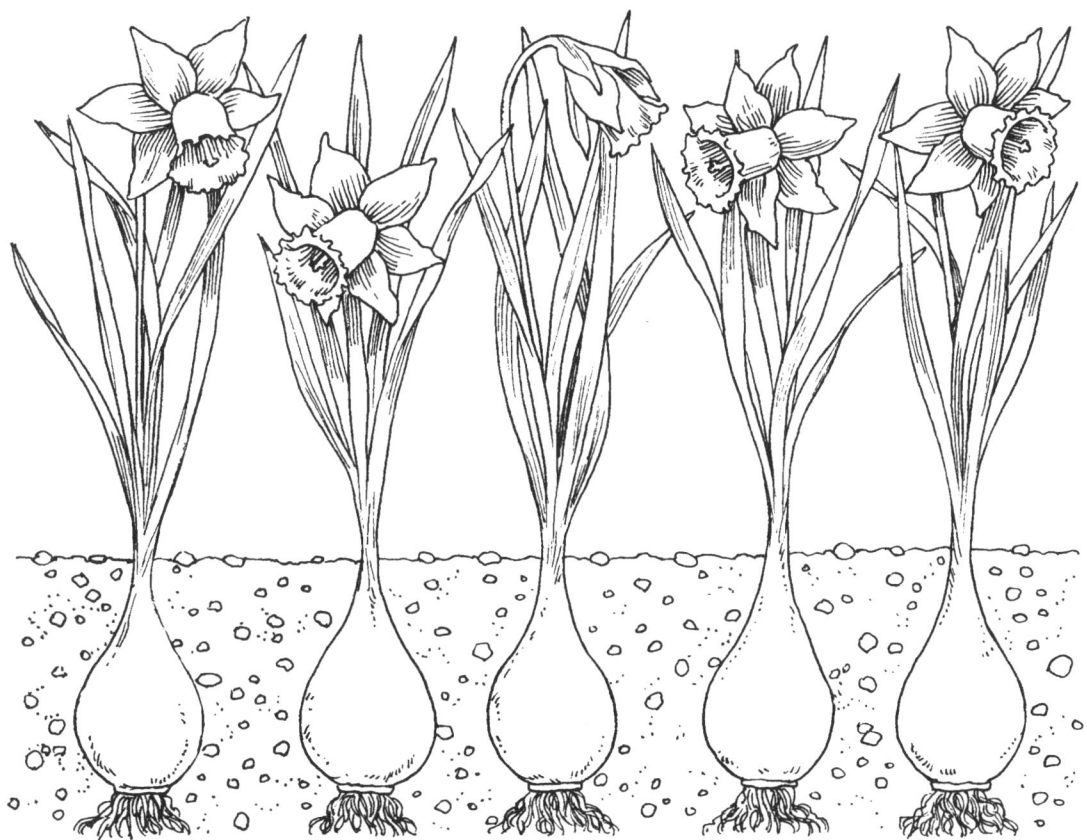

Friends, family and beyond

We often take for granted relationships which are so much part of our everyday lives that we hardly notice them, yet we all depend on each other in very many ways. Parents, brothers and sisters, grand-parents, cousins, aunts and uncles, all play a part in our general wellbeing. We may also belong to groups beyond the family such as school, college, clubs and associations. Further afield we belong to the wider community of the town or village where we live.

In the diagram on the Focus Page opposite, Danny has charted all the people who affect his life and put them into groups. Sometimes the groups over-lap; his sister and step-brother go to the same school and share some friends; the whole family belong to the city cycling club. Some groups are particularly close to Danny; he writes regularly to his uncle in Canada who is a great friend. Others are more remote; he rarely sees or writes to his aunt in London. In the space on the Focus Page or on a larger piece of paper design your own relationship chart over-lapping circles and putting groups near or far from the centre as appropriate to you.

When you have finished, take time to look at each group in turn, reflecting on how they affect your life and what aspect there is to be thankful for.

- Are there daily chores which your immediate family do such as cleaning, cooking, earning the money for you all?

- Are there ways your family encourage and support you?
- Are there times when you are glad of their forgiveness and tolerance?
- How about your extended family?
- Are you aware of times when you have enjoyed knowing you have a wider family?

- What do you appreciate about your particular friends?
- Do you belong to a club or association?
- What do you enjoy about this?

How about the community where you live? For a moment consider the daily commitment of local councils, doctors, police, community workers and employ-ees of public services such as road clean-ing, water, gas and electricity. These people all play an often unrecognised part in our daily lives.

- Do you think that it matters whether people are thanked for their contribu-tion to the general life of the group? Why do you think this?
- Does your awareness of the work and effort of others change the way you act in the community?
- Do you feel we all have a part to play in friendships, families, schools, clubs and communities?

Can you think of occasions when it might be appropriate to express thankfulness?

Friends, family and beyond

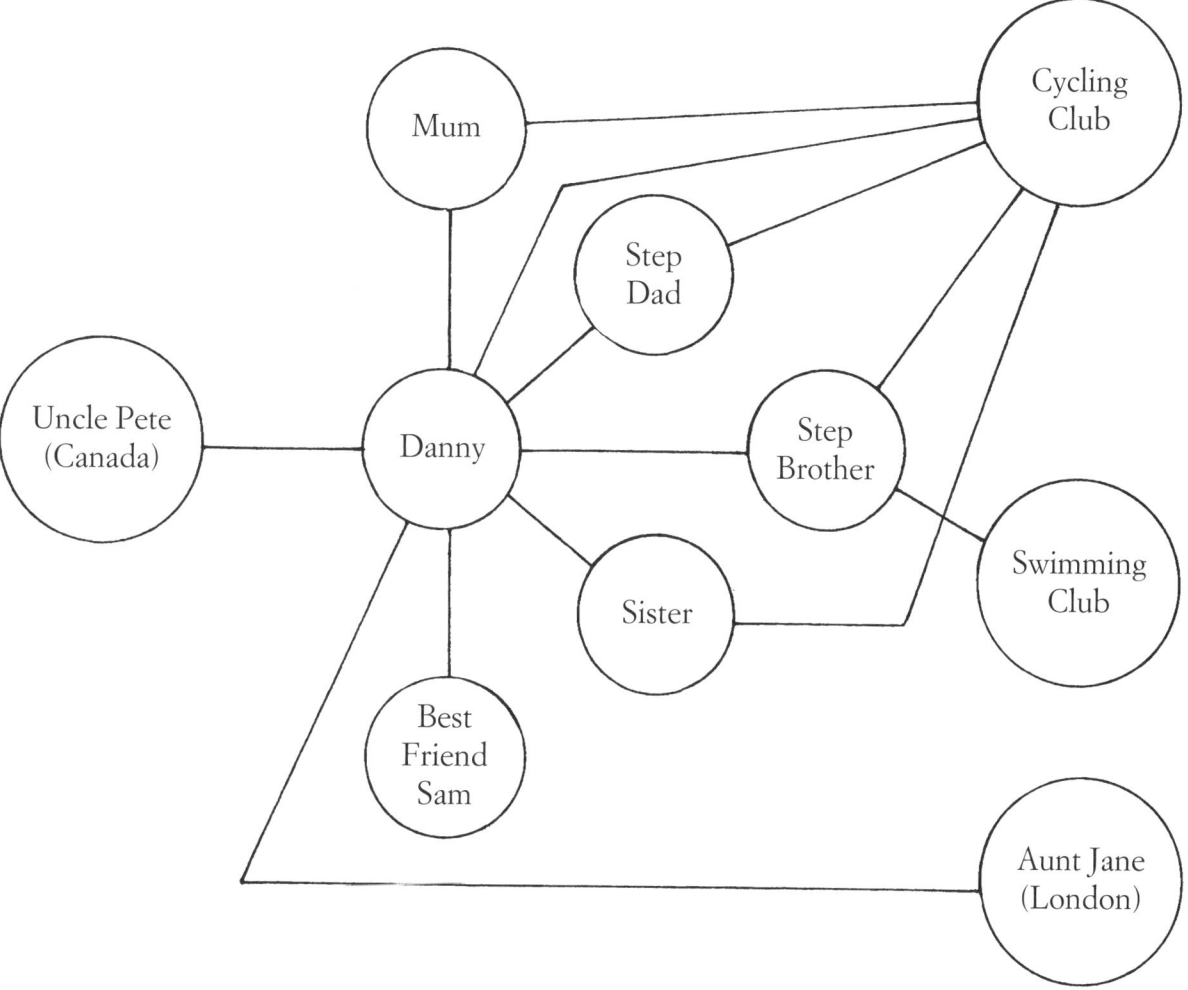

Third Prayer Mood
ATTENTIVE LISTENING

Have you ever longed for a friend who would listen to your deepest hopes and fears without judging you or interrupting or offering unwanted advice?

Such friends are a rare and precious gift. Many people only listen with 'half an ear' whilst their real attention is elsewhere. Listening attentively is a great skill and if we are to become a good friend to ourselves and to others we need to develop the skill of attentive listening, listening with the whole of our being.

This is not always easy as listening may mean facing up to realities which we can easily hide by frenzied activity and noise. It is in stillness and silence that we can listen and become more aware of our deepest hopes and fears and gradually find the courage to see the path forward. This will only happen if we make time to stop and listen. The following Prayer Focus pages are to help you to listen to yourself, to others, and in prayer to develop the skill of attending to 'the small still voice'. Prayer Focus 9 looks at 'listening' to the daily events of your life by keeping a Journal. Prayer Focus 10 examines the use of 'daydreaming' as a way of opening up and listening to our imagination and hopes for our lives. Prayer Focus 11, 'Learning to listen', and Prayer Focus 12, 'Headlines', are more practical, giving suggestions to help develop good listening skills and to use them in daily situations such as watching the TV News.

Journals and diaries

Keeping a diary can be a way of enjoying a friend who is always there for you to listen and will not interrupt!

Anne Frank, who kept a diary whilst in hiding during the Second World War, wrote of her own diary:

I am grateful to God for giving me this gift . . . of expressing all that is in me . . . I hope I will be able to confide in you completely . . . and I hope you will be a great support and comfort to me.

The habit of spending perhaps 5 to 10 minutes 'considering' and reflecting on the day is a valuable way of putting life in perspective and gaining understanding about the way we are choosing to live our lives. Trying to pin down in words the main atmosphere of the day helps us to acknowledge our feelings, our successes and failures and to perhaps see a way forward. Diaries are also a tangible record of our life's journey. It is possible to look back at former entries and realise that we have felt miserable and abandoned before and come through the experience, and that we have been disappointed before and found new hope.

This kind of 'journaling' is very different in purpose from keeping a Filofax! It is not the place for noting down appointments or jotting memos. It is the place where reflections about events, feelings, hopes and fears can be expressed. It is a place for confessions and confidences, for developing dreams which may at present be too frail and unformed to be spoken. It can also be a place to record special events or to note down quotations or accounts of books, films or videos which have affected you. However, the purpose of the record is not primarily a blow-by-blow description of the event but rather an exploration of what it meant to you.

The passage on the Focus Page perhaps explains this more clearly:

Notice how the *italicised* passages reflect on the feelings around the event. By reflecting and writing in the diary Maggie is able to acknowledge what is going on at a different level to the actual outside events and grows in self-awareness and understanding of others. She is able to bring to the surface 'negative' feelings which might otherwise have festered and to recognise and record the affirming experiences of the day which can be part of a memory bank of self-worth.

How to begin your diary

Choose a hard-backed notebook with lined or plain pages but no dates. You may like to put a cover on the book and decorate it. This is your private and personal property so find somewhere safe to keep it. You can record whatever you want; you may choose to keep the contents entirely private or sometimes to share them with a special friend or person in the family. Each day try to spend 5 to 10 minutes reflecting on the day and noting down what is significant for you and what you are feeling. You may like to stick mementoes in your diary: a flower picked on a special walk, a ticket to a football match, a newspaper report of a school concert.

Journals and diaries

Today was my sixteenth birthday. Mum brought me breakfast in bed; something that only ever happens on red letter days or when I'm ill! There was even a rose in a vase on the tray and my cards were piled up by the mug of coffee. *I felt really special.*

Dan, my older brother, came in with his present. It was a tape of my favourite group. I was so pleased. *He gave me a hug when he put the parcel down. We don't always get on and suddenly I felt really close to him.* My little sister arrived next. She had bought me a china ornament for my dressing table. She wanted to get in bed beside me and open all my cards. *She is so cute and I do love her but today I wanted to enjoy the luxury of breakfast in bed and to be honest I felt quite irritable with her. I hope she didn't notice. She was trying to be loving.* We were so busy looking at the cards that we didn't realise the time. I leapt out of bed, washed and dressed, grabbed my school things, but although Dad took a short cut in the car I knew I would be late. Miss Turnball is really strict, sarcastic sometimes, and as I opened the door to the classroom I dreaded her response. But my friend Sally had told her that it was my birthday and to my amazement she said, 'Happy birthday, Maggie' and actually smiled. *D'you know she looks quite human when she smiles? I couldn't help wondering if anyone ever brought her breakfast in bed or gave her a hug. Suddenly I saw her in a different way. I've decided to try to be nicer to her in the future.*

Concluding Reflection

When you have finished writing your entry for the day read it through. What has been important to you? What has your mood been?

If it has been a mood of happiness, do you want to share that thanksgiving with anyone?

If it is a mood of anger or annoyance is there anything you need to do to help you feel more at peace ?

If it is a mood of anxiety or worry do you need help from anyone? Where can you go for help?

Dreams of life

Some people believe that daydreaming is a waste of time, but often when we allow ourselves time to dream we enter a different level of understanding and we can discover our deepest needs and hopes. Allow yourself time to dream and time to consider if you want your dream to come true.

Read these instructions before you begin the exercise;

1 Find a place where you can be quiet and uninterrupted. Find a position in which you can sit or lie down comfortably with your neck and head supported. Make sure that your clothes are comfortable and that you are neither too warm or too cold.

2 Read the 'River of life' introduction on Focus Page 10 and choose one of the dreams as your focus. Read the introduction and the chosen dream through carefully several times until you can visualise it for yourself.

3 Put the book down and relax completely. Become aware of the rhythm of your breathing. When you feel ready, close your eyes and picture the 'River of life' dream. You could even tape the dream description and play it back, imagining you are there as you listen. Do not hurry. Stop at places where you feel the need to reflect.

4 At the end of the dream open your eyes slowly and bring yourself back into the room.

When you have completed the exercise reflect on the dream by asking questions like these:

• What did you like about the boat in the dream you chose?
• Would you like to try any of the other boats?
• Would you prefer to be on a river or stream or at sea?
• Do you like business and activity or stillness and peace.
• Does the comfort of the boat matter to you?
• Would you rather be alone or in company with others?
• Does it matter to you if you are going somewhere or just having fun?

Let your answers to these questions tell you something about the kind of person you are. Then think about the voyage of life which lies ahead of you:

• Where do you want to go?
• What do you want to do?
• Are there any gifts of personality which God has given you which will influence your life's choices and direction?
• On any voyage you will need a map, a compass, food for the journey, knowledge of where to turn and what to do when you are lost or in danger. Where can you find these things for the voyage of life?
• Do you have a sense of direction in which you want to go?
• Do you have a set of values to steer by and a faith to see you through?

Dreams of life

Introduction to the 'River of life' dreams
You are sitting on the bank of a river under the shade of a tree and you can see far into the distance, much further than usual. To your left the river joins the wide-open sea stretching to the horizon. Your gaze follows the contour of the coastline and not far away you see a pier and the harbour of a small seaside town. To your right you follow the course of the river back into the hills, flowing through fields, towns and villages and joined by smaller tributaries and streams which glide beneath weeping willow trees or tumble over rocks on the steep hillsides.

Dream 1
A tug turns into the river from the sea. It is loaded with tarpaulin-covered boxes and the pilot is guiding it up river to an industrial town. As it ties up at the dock you can hear the noise of traffic and machinery, and the shouting of the dockers as a crane hoists the load from the tug onto the quayside. A forklift truck takes the boxes into a warehouse.

Dream 2
You can see far back up river where it is a fast-flowing stream. A canoeist is on the bank packing the canoe with food and a small tent before sliding it into the water and climbing in. Testing skill and courage the canoeist steers to mid-stream and starts to paddle towards the rapids.

Dream 3
Looking to the left you see a pleasure boat tied up against the seaside pier, its flags fluttering in the breeze. Adults and children are crowding onto the boat and laughing as it rocks on the waves. Loud music plays from a radio and the boat sets off to the happy cheers of the passengers.

Dream 4
To your left beyond the pier a vast liner is moving slowly towards the horizon. You can even see the people on board. The captain is looking at his charts and the crew are busy about their duties. But the passengers are thinking and talking happily of far-off places. Dream with them.

Dream 5
You look towards the harbour and see a fishing boat moored alongside the quay. The crew are checking their tackle and equipment. You can hear them talking about their experiences – rough voyages with treacherous seas, sailing at night under the stars.

Dream 6
Nearby on the river you hear the regular splash of a rowing boat going by. Two young children in life jackets are enjoying the fun as their mum and dad pull at the oars. There is a picnic basket in the boat and they are heading for an island further upstream.

Dream 7
A large speedboat whizzes by close to the shore. It looks very expensive and is fitted with all the latest equipment. The people on board are fashionably dressed and obviously enjoying their luxurious lifestyle, not to mention the envy and admiration of onlookers.

Learning to listen

Can you remember a time when you needed to tell someone something important and really wanted them to listen carefully to what you wanted to say? Listening is an important skill. The following exercise is to help you to develop your own skills in listening. To do this exercise you need to work in pairs, so you will need to ask a friend or member of the family to co-operate.

Sit with your partner in chairs facing each other. Take a few minutes in silence to decide on an event or experience you want to tell your partner about. Then decide who will be *First Speaker* and who will be *First Listener*.

When the *First Speaker* has finished, the *Listener* then tells the event back to the *Speaker*. When that is completed the *First Speaker* discusses with the *Listener* how it felt to be listened to.

- How accurate was the *Listener's* account of the event?

- Did the *Listener* note how the *Speaker* was feeling as well as what was being said?

- What behaviour of the *Listener* helped the *Speaker* to continue with the story?

- What behaviour of the *Listener* distracted the *Speaker* from continuing the account?

- Did the way the *Listener* looked or sat make any difference?

Now repeat the exercise with the *First Speaker* taking a turn at listening and discuss the experience as above. Remember that the aim of the exercise is to help each other to listen better. Try to make your remarks to each other as positive and helpful as possible. For example; 'It really helped me when you looked at me but when you looked out of the window I felt you weren't interested in what I was saying', rather than; 'You weren't listening you were looking out of the window!'

Together make a list of helpful listening skills and unhelpful listening behaviour. Compare your list with the list on the Focus Page.

Are there any similarities or differences? Can you put these skills into practice next time someone wants to speak with you?

Learning to listen

Unhelpful behaviour would be:

- showing boredom or ridicule

- fiddling or looking at your watch

- interrupting or talking too much

- criticising the speaker

- looking away or fidgeting in your chair

The good listener generally:

- gives undivided attention

- makes eye contact with the person who is speaking but without staring.

- smiles or looks sympathetic to what is being said

- shows by the way they are sitting that they are attending

- asks questions which help the speaker to continue

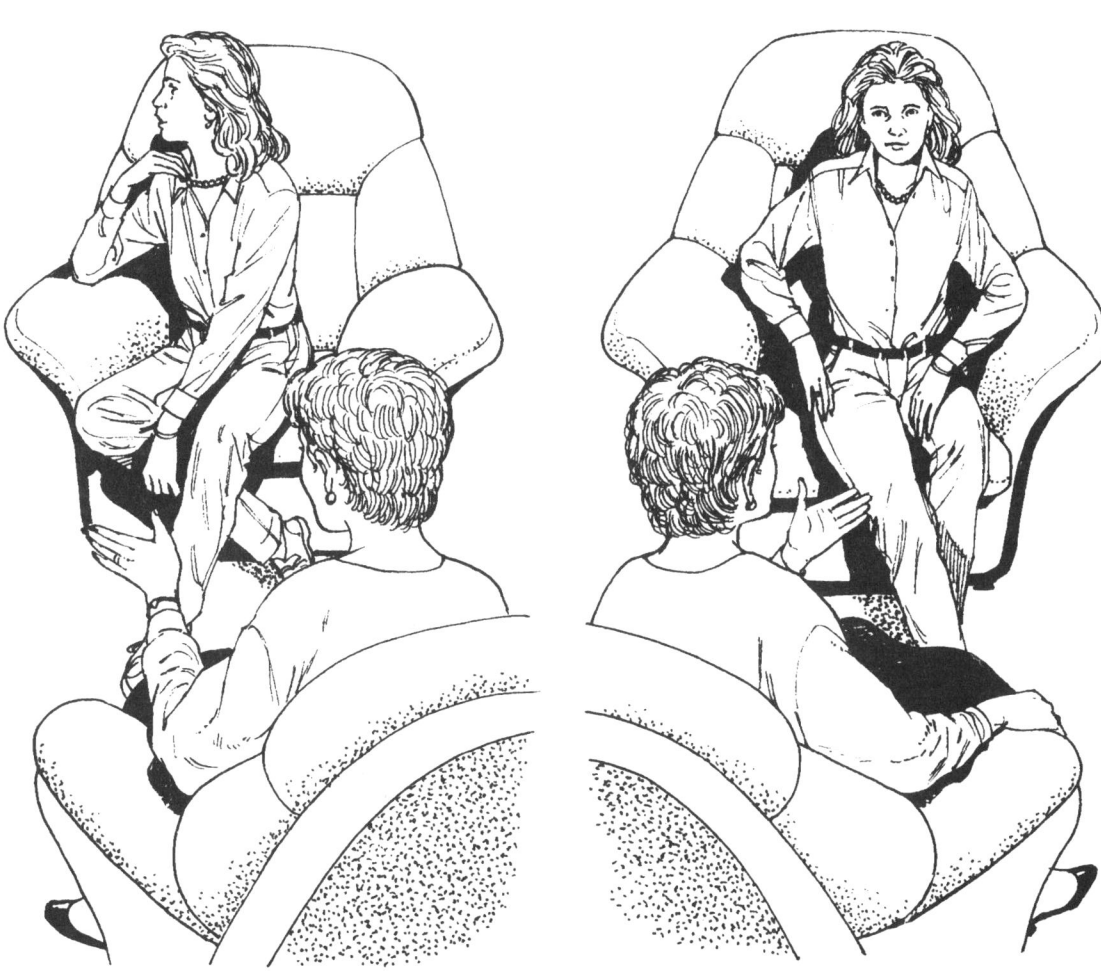

Headlines

Do you ever watch the evening news on television? Are you ever aware of how much you can remember at the end of the broadcast?

This exercise is to help you to attend and listen in a way which will enhance your listening skills.

Decide in advance on an evening to watch one of the news bulletins. Check that it does not clash with a meal time or a time when other members of the family want to watch a special programme. Make sure that you are sitting ready for the programme to begin and have the television tuned to the right channel. Have with you a pen or pencil ready for the end of the broadcast.

While you are watching the news make sure you are also listening to what is being said. Attend to the main headlines:

- How many headlines are there?
- What are the main stories?
- Are they of conflict or celebration? Political events or environmental issues?
- Who are the main people interviewed? Politicians? Stars of the sports or media world? Local people who witnessed a particular event?
- Do the pictures being shown actually correspond to what is being said? (Be aware of what you are 'listening' to – the words or the picture!)

It may help you to keep a count of how many main issues are covered.

When the broadcast ends, turn the television off or if this is not possible go into another room. Using the blank 'newspaper page' on Focus Page 12 fill in the main news headlines and personalities, sketching in some illustrations or scenes which were vivid to you.

Reflect on your feelings as you heard the news:

- Did you listen to what was said?
- Did you 'listen' to the body language of the people speaking?
- Do you think the reporter or interviewer listened carefully enough?
- How far did the pictures of what you saw affect you?
- Did the pictures affect you more than the words?
- Were there events you felt strongly about?
- Were there events you would have liked more information about?
- Did you think that the news item which was most important received the most coverage?
- Were there events which you felt you wanted to act upon?
- What could you do to influence events by the way you choose to live and behave?

Headlines

Daily News & Views

35p

Fourth Prayer Mood

WONDER AND WORSHIP

Sometimes, experiences in life can lead us to wonder and worship with complete spontaneity. It could be that the awesome sight of mountains or the miracle of a new-born baby can suddenly awaken in us a sense of the miraculous and the awareness that 'it's a wonderful world'. Sometimes the generous kindness or amazing courage of others can inspire us to respond with a real desire to follow the commandment to love God 'with all your heart, with all your soul, with all your mind and with all your strength' (Mark 12:30).

The following exercises are designed to help us to become more aware of the miraculous and to consider how we might respond. Prayer Focus 13, 'The viewfinder', helps us to focus more accurately on the world around us whilst Focus 14, 'Space and time', draws attention to the awesomeness of our place in the created universe. Prayer Focus 15, 'The prison cell', looks at the ways in which we may refuse to experience beauty and mystery and how we block the opportunities of wonder. The concluding Focus of this section, 'What can I give?', reflects on how our attitude of worship and wonder may lead us to share our gifts and become involved in loving and serving those around us.

PRAYER FOCUS 13

The viewfinder

If you are a photographer you will know how choosing the focus for your picture can make you look at your surroundings in a new way. What is near? What is in the distance? What should be included in the frame? What should be omitted? What is the light like? What effect do you want to achieve?

During the day our eyes look at and glance at many 'views', yet we do not always attend to what we see. Take some time alone to find a 'view' on which to focus for five minutes. It could be the view from your bedroom window or across the kitchen. You may decide to take a small object like a fir cone, a stone or a flower. Look carefully, attending to the detail. What do you notice? Be aware of different shades of light, of texture, of pattern. Be aware of the objects in your 'viewfinder'. If your 'viewfinder' includes a scene with people in it notice who they are, what they are wearing, how they are behaving. You may become aware of small acts of kindness which you observe. Your 'viewfinder' may choose an animal. Can you notice its fur, its habits, the way it moves?

On the Focus Page are two 'Views' which may help you to get the idea. One is focusing with a wide 'viewfinder' on the experience of watching for the dawn, the other is looking with a smaller range 'viewfinder' and focusing on a stone.

Concluding Reflection

What did your 'viewfinder' choose?
What did you observe?
What were your feelings?
Was there anything you saw which could be a cause for wonder or worship?
Were you aware of how many things you pass by without noticing in your everyday life?
Could you make a habit of taking a minute a day to 'stand and stare'?
Could you keep a sketch pad to jot down in words or pictures something which 'caught your eye' each day?
Could you keep a 'Worship and Wonder' diary in which you note down things you have noticed? This could also include poems or passages from books which have led other people to worship and wonder.
Does the exercise of worship and wonder lead you to action?

Concluding Prayer

Open our eyes that we may see the glory all around us.
Lift up the shutters which obscure the wonder which surrounds us.
Amen.

The viewfinder

Mary looked around her; there was nothing but darkness. They had agreed to meet here on the hill near the ruins of the old cathedral to watch the dawn. But now as she stood alone she wondered if anyone else would come; indeed she wondered about the sun ever rising again as she stood peering into the gloom. It was a still, black night and even if she focused her eyes purposefully she could only just perceive the walls of the ruins and the outline of a tree which she knew were there. There was no moon and not a twinkling of a star in the sky, but quite against all the odds an unseen bird sang.

There was a rustling and she turned to see a shape which gradually changed into an outline of a woman walking towards her out of the greyness. Then she saw: coming from all directions people were walking up the hill, alone, in pairs, some carrying children still sleepy and wrapped against the early morning chill. They gathered together in silence, their faces straining towards the east.

Mary could never explain when or how it happened. It was imperceptible, like breathing, like the opening of blossom on a tree or the movement of the wind across a field of wheat. There was a change in the colour of the horizon, a paler shade of black, a paler shade of grey and then the lines upon lines of red and pink and even streaks of delicate eggshell blue across the sky. It took her by surprise when she realised that the outline of the trees on the hill were now silhouetted clearly against the sky and the faces of previously anonymous figures became recognisable as her friends. The walls of the ruins became solid stone and wondrously colour was restored: the green of the grass beneath her feet, the shining yellow of a child's wellington boot, the dancing blue of someone's eyes. Light had returned with the dawning of the day. It was Easter.

Paul had intended to skim the stone across the waves when he first picked it up, but as he turned it preparing for the throw he had become aware of its shape and texture and the tiny cracks in its surface. Glancing down he saw that it was not one uniform colour but made up of a darker and lighter brown which showed an amazing range of shades changing as the stone dried in the warmth of his hand. Examining it more closely he observed the patterns on it. On one side it looked almost like a ram's head and on the other he could almost discern a face.

How had this stone been formed? By what upheavals of the earth and batterings of the sea had it reached its present form? How long had it been on this beach? How many people had trodden over it without noticing? What other person had held it in their hands as he did now. He looked out at the rise and fall of the waves, wondering.

Space and time

The person who wrote the Psalms often reflected with awe on the created world and the wonder of the God revealed in Creation:

'The heavens are telling the glory of God and the firmament proclaims his handiwork' (Psalm 19:1).

The writer also marvelled that the God who had created the heavens and earth was also concerned about humanity. Confronted with the vastness and enormity of the created world the Psalmist grappled with the amazing belief that this same God was infinitely loving and involved with humankind: 'When I look at the heavens, the moon and the stars which God created, how is it that God is concerned with me and cares for me?' (Adapted from Psalm 8.)

The Psalmist was also full of wonder that this God of Creation also moved through time and space, that there was nowhere God's presence could not reach and no point in time or history which was not under God's all-encompassing love:

'You search out my path and know all my ways. Even before a word is on my tongue you know it altogether. If I ascend to the heavens you are there, if I take the wings of the morning and go to the uttermost parts of the sea you are there also.' (Adapted from Psalm 139.)

- Have you ever stopped to wonder at your place in time and space?

- Where do you fit in within history and time?

- What events do you know about which happened before you were born?

Within living memory? Within this century? During last century? Within the last two thousand years? Before the birth of Christ? Before recorded history?

- What events do you know happened after you were born? Before you went to school? Before you were eleven? In the last year?

- Where do you fit in within the created world?

- What created forces are larger than you physically?

- What creatures are larger than you physically?

- What aspects of creation are smaller than you physically? What aspects of creation are smaller than you physically but more powerful?

- Where do you see yourself in creation and do you have a role?

In the space on the Focus Page use your imagination to develop a picture, pattern or design showing how you see your place in time and space and your relationship to the created world. You may like to transfer the ideas onto your computer.

Concluding Reflection

'I am the Alpha and the Omega', says the Lord God, who is and who was and who is to come, the Almighty. I am the Alpha and the Omega, the first and the last, the beginning and the end.' (Adapted from Revelation 1:8 and 22:13.)

Space and time

The prison cell

Sometimes we read of people who have been kidnapped and held in a confined space or a cell for a long time. In these dreadful and restricting situations, when the ordinary experiences of life are denied, people sometimes become even more sensitive to the incredible beauty and opportunities of life. Paradoxically many of us who enjoy freedom live unaware of the beauty around us, failing to appreciate the fullness of life and choosing to disregard or under-develop our gifts. We may even build our own prison walls preventing ourselves from using our potential and becoming part of the wonder of life.

If you were imprisoned what would you miss most:
• Space to move? A distant view?
• Food? A hot bath?
• Companionship of friends?
• Books? Television? Computer?
• Freedom to choose?
• A sense of pattern to the day?

Allow yourself time to reflect with wonder on the freedoms you enjoy.
  Jesus said: 'I have come in order that you might have life – life in all its fullness.' (John 10:10; Good News Bible.)

• What do you think he meant by this?
• Do you deny yourself 'life in all its fullness' and 'imprison' yourself?
• Do you develop all your talents?
• Do you take opportunities to wonder at the created world?
• Do you appreciate friends and family?

• Do you find yourself using phrases like 'I'd love to, but . . .'? 'I'd like to, but I couldn't because . . .'?

Look carefully at your reasons for not doing something.
• Are the reasons based on care for others, realistic assessment of your responsibilities and abilities?
• Are they based on lack of initiative? Fear of being noticed? Fear of failing, succeeding or what others think?

Do you use these phrases:
• 'I haven't enough money/time'
• '. . . wouldn't allow me to'
• 'I'm not clever enough'
• 'I haven't got the right experience'
• 'I don't like to ask for help'?

Do these attitudes block opportunities for worship and wonder? Are there ways in which you can unlock the door to your cell and be alive to worship and wonder?

Concluding Prayer

God our creator who loves all you
    have made.
Grant us courage and faith to
    unlock all the doors which would
    bar us from the fullness of life
    you wish us to enjoy.
Then let us live to love and serve
    with worship and wonder.
    Amen.

The prison cell

Here is a picture of the high brick walls of a cell in which there is a locked door. On the bricks of the wall write the reasons which you believe prevent you from living life 'to the full'. Remember to include some of your attitudes.

Can you fill in the following sentence?

'If I could be free and out of this cell I could . . .

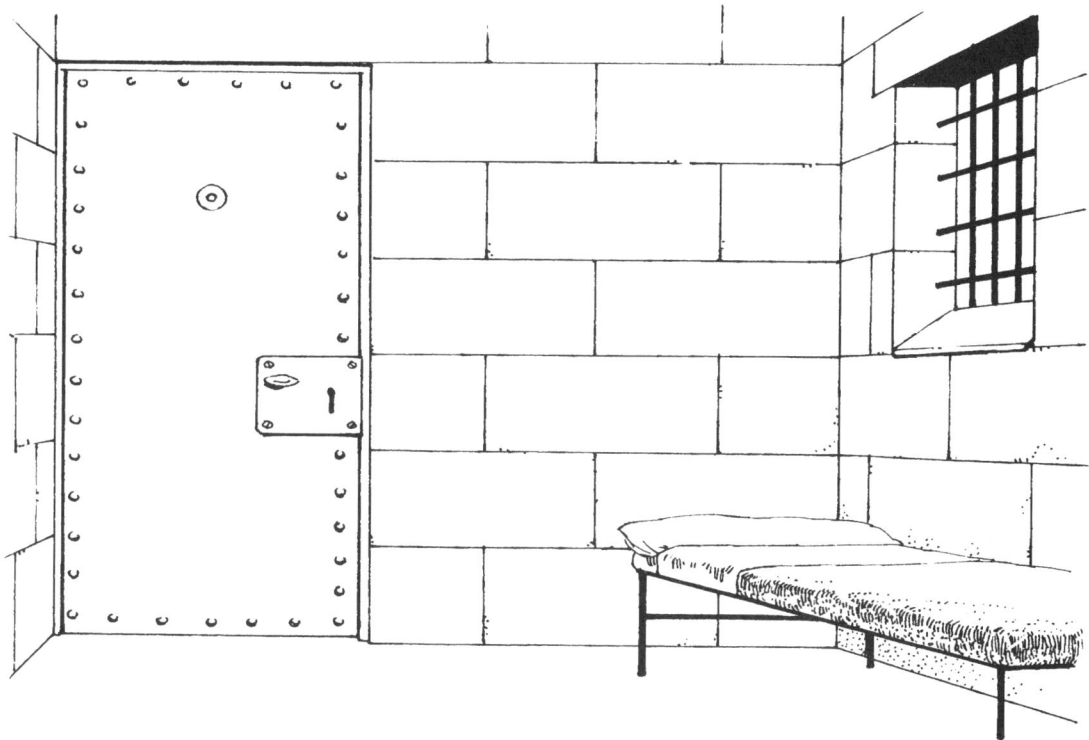

Here is the key to unlock the door to your cell:

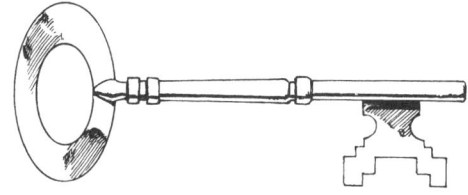

Complete the following sentence:

'To lift the key and open the door of my cell I must . . .

Will you choose to do this?

PRAYER FOCUS 16

What can I give?

Sometimes an increasing awareness of the wonder of the world around us, and of the gifts of life and health which we enjoy, can bring us to a greater sense of our responsibilities to the world and a real desire to love and serve others, and to use the abundance of our own opportunities to enrich the lives of others.

The following poems capture something of that mood of wanting to respond to wonder in service and love:

This is our God, the Servant King,
   he calls us now to follow him,
   to bring our lives as a daily offering
   of worship to the Servant King.

What can I give him, poor as I am?
If I were a shepherd I would bring a
   lamb;
     if I were a wise man I would do my
      part;
     yet what I can I give him – give my
      heart.

Read the story, 'The gift', on the Focus Page and then take time to reflect on the story. It is not a story of the wonder of the natural world but rather how sometimes injustice and the vulnerability of people can lead us to a sense of wonder and gratitude and a desire to serve others.

- What were Stuart and Richard able to offer?
- What did other people offer?
- Were the offerings very different?
- What do you feel you would want to give as your offering?

Your unique skill can be a way of worshipping and an offering to God. Try to set aside a time each week to develop your gift and reflect on how you can share your giftedness with others in the spirit of worship and praise.

Concluding Prayer

Yours, Lord, is the greatness, the power,
   the glory, the splendour, and the majesty;
   for everything in heaven and on earth is
   yours.
All things come from you,
   and of your own do we give you.
   (ASB, page 129.)

What can I give?

The gift

Stuart and Richard were laughing as they walked home together through the park, chatting about the orchestra rehearsal. It had gone well and they were looking forward to performing in the concert in a few weeks' time.

As they neared the centre of the park they came upon the old man who was a familiar feature of the park for them both. He was known in the area as 'Old Bill'. He was always on the same bench, curled up with his navy woollen hat pulled well down over his ears, his plastic carriers tucked under the bench. Most days people walked by him without a glance. Those who did turn their head often showed disapproval as if his presence was disreputable and unwelcome.

But this night something had changed.

Perhaps it was the sudden coldness of the weather that aroused people's awareness, or maybe the report on the TV news of a man found frozen and near to death had prompted their conscience. Whatever the reason, Stuart and Richard noticed the difference on that Tuesday evening.

To begin with, the old man was sitting upright. A woman who lived in one of the large houses opposite the park had brought Bill an old sleeping bag and he was wrapping it around himself. A businessman on his way home had bought a couple of hot dogs from the stall at the park entrance and the old man was munching them. Even the park gardener who was generally bad-tempered had found him a piece of plastic sheeting to keep out the rain. As they were about to walk by, Stuart's glance met the eyes of the old man and suddenly, and for the first time, he was aware of what it might be like to be alone and cold, hungry and with no one to care whether one lived or died. He was acutely aware of the sheer richness of his own life: the hot meal he knew he would eat that evening, the warmth of a hot bath and the shelter of a home against the searing wind. His heart was full of gratitude for all that he received and he wished he had something to give Old Bill, but neither of them had anything to offer for food or shelter.

Suddenly Stuart had an idea. They were carrying their violins under their arms and the music of the rehearsal was still singing in their ears. Stuart whispered his plan to Richard. They got out their instruments and somewhat nervously Richard announced to Bill: 'This is a concert just for you.' They had been learning a medley of popular tunes from the Beatles hits. Soon they were in the swing: *All you need is love, When I'm 64, Lucy in the sky with diamonds* . . . As they played they noticed that Bill was tapping his foot and even singing along. At times he even smiled.

When they had finished he gave a quiet round of applause and then went back to munching his sandwich. The boys put their instruments away. 'It was the best we could offer,' said Stuart.

45

Fifth Prayer Mood

INTERCEDING

Interceding is a way of laying our needs and the needs of our communities and the wider world before the loving presence of God. We do so in the assurance that 'God is for us' and wants peace and fullness of life for us.

Jesus always spoke of God as a loving parent who was concerned with humanity and wanted to meet their needs. He describes God as someone who is aware of our needs:

Therefore do not be anxious, saying, 'What shall we eat?' or 'What shall we drink?' or 'What shall we wear?' . . . your heavenly father knows that you need them all. Matthew 6:31, 32

Jesus reassured his disciples, telling them to make their needs known to God:

And I tell you, 'Ask, and it will be given you; seek, and you will find; knock and it will be opened to you. For everyone who asks receives, and he who seeks finds, and to him who knocks it will be opened.' Luke 11:9-10

Yet opening our hopes and fears before God can be risky; we may find that we are being asked to look at what we need to do to love and care for those in need and to consider how the way we act and behave affects the lives of those around us. Intercession can bring challenge, conflict and new responsibilities as well as the reassurance of God's presence with us.

The following Prayer Focus pages explore different ways of interceding. Prayer Focus 17, 'What's in the paper?', and Prayer Focus 18, 'What's on the news tonight?', use the media as a way into prayer; Prayer Focus 19 uses a candle as a focus for meditative intercession whilst Prayer Focus 20 uses the imagery of a pebble thrown into a pool to help us explore the issues of personal responsibility.

PRAYER FOCUS 17

What's in the paper?

As you travel on a bus or train, or sit in the dentist's waiting room, you may observe many people looking at a daily paper. They may be reading a complicated report or merely flicking through the pictures. Looking at a newspaper can be a reflective way of alerting oneself to the needs of the world and becoming aware of the contrasts between the kind of 'kingdom' of which Jesus frequently spoke and the world in which we live.

Look through the newspaper. As you turn from page to page notice each article and picture. Which events in the world cause you sorrow, anxiety, excitement, pleasure, hope, pain? You may like to use the imaginary newspaper pages on the Focus Page to start with, but try to find a daily paper and include this exercise at least once a week.

When you have looked through the newspaper for the first time choose one article or picture to focus on. Now imagine that you are looking at the pictures or articles in the presence of God:

- What is God saying about these issues?
- Are there issues where you feel you would like to be involved?
- What could you do to help?
- Are there occasions when there is nothing you can do?
- How does that make you feel?
- What can you do with those feelings?
- Do you think Jesus ever felt powerless?
- What did he do when he felt isolated?
- Can you share your feelings with God in prayer?

Concluding Reflection

God, grant me the serenity
    to accept the things I cannot change,
    the courage to change the things I can
    and the wisdom to know the difference.
(Prayer by Reinhold Niebuhr.)

What's in the paper?

What's on the news tonight?

Jesus made it clear in his teaching and behaviour that belief in a loving God also implied a responsibility to carry God's love and care into the communities around us. He spoke of serving God by serving those in need or distress. This is especially clear in the passage in Saint Matthew's Gospel 25:31-46:

I was hungry and you gave me food;
I was thirsty and you gave me drink;
I was a foreigner and you took me home
*   with you;*
I was in rags and you gave me clothes;
I fell ill and you looked after me;
I was in prison and you came to see me.
Believe me – when you helped the least
*   of my brothers you helped me.*

(From *New World. The Heart of the New Testament in Plain English*. Alan T. Dale. OUP.)

Make a decision to watch one of the TV news programmes completely and to attend to each issue. As each news item appears, try to commend the people into God's care. At the end try to remember the main points of the broadcast. Are there areas where your action could help? Are there issues on which you need to find out more to understand what is going on? Are there events in which you want to voice an opinion or become involved?

There are many organisations which work to serve those in need. On the focus page is a selection of some of them. What do you know about their work? Perhaps you could find out about an organisation which works in an area which particularly concerns you. You may like to make an effort to remember their work regularly in your time of reflection.

Concluding Reflection

Christ has no body now on earth but yours,
    no hands but yours,
    no feet but yours.
Yours are the eyes through which must look
    out Christ's compassion on the world.
Yours are the feet with which he is to go
    about doing good.
Yours are the hands with which he is to
    bless men now. Amen.
    (Prayer of Saint Teresa.)

But be doers of the word and not merely
    hearers.
    (James 1:22.)

What's on the news tonight?

Amnesty International
1 Easton Street, London WC1X 8DJ. Tel: 0171-413 5500

Catholic Fund for Overseas Development (CAFOD)
2 Romero Close, Stockwell Road, London SW9 9TY

Christian Aid
PO Box 100, London SE1 7RT. Tel: 0171-620 4444

Church Action on Poverty
Central Buildings, Oldham Street, Manchester M1 1JT. Tel: 0161-236 9321

Friends of the Earth
26 Underwood Street, London N1 7JQ. Tel: 0171-490 1555

Oxfam
274 Banbury Road, Oxford OX2 7DZ. Tel: 01865 311311

Help the Aged
St James' Walk, Clerkenwell, London EC1R 0BE. Tel: 0171-895 1407

Royal Association in Aid of Deaf People
27 Old Oak Road, Acton, London W3 7HN. Tel: 0181-743 6187

Quaker Peace and Service
Friends House, Euston Road, London NW1 2BJ. Tel: 0171-387 3601

Save the Children Fund
17 Grove Lane, Camberwell, London SE25 8RD. Tel: 0171-703 5400

Shelter
88 Old Street, London EC1V 9HU. Tel: 0171-253 0202

Tear Fund
100 Church Road, Teddington, Middlesex TW11 8QE. Tel: 0181-977 9144

The Children's Society
Edward Rudolf House, 69 Margery Street, London WC1X 0JL. Tel: 0171-837 4299

Traidcraft
Kingsway, Gateshead NE11 0NE. Tel: 0191-491 0591

The candle

Sometimes there is a particular problem which worries us or a person we love is ill and we feel anxious or concerned. It may be that we do not know what to do or perhaps feel there is nothing we *can* do.

The following exercise is to help us to bring this issue into the loving presence of God, trusting his guidance and strength.

SAFETY NOTE

Make sure that you are very careful when using candles. Always place them in a secure holder where they cannot be knocked over. Make sure they are away from anything which might catch alight and have some water or a fire blanket available for emergencies. Never leave a room with a candle burning unattended.

Find a place where you can be alone and uninterrupted. Choose a stout candle and place it in a sturdy holder which will not fall over. Put this at a level where you can sit and see it comfortably.

As you light the candle remember the words Jesus said: 'I am the light of the world.'

Sit quietly and focus your attention on the candle, watching how the light spreads around it. Observe how it sometimes flickers and sometimes leaps up with new energy. What do you notice about it particularly?

Reflect on the person or situation you feel needs bringing to the light of Christ. Imagine the warmth and comfort of God's love reaching out to that person. Think about the light of reassurance shining in the dark places of fear and doubt. Visualise the light illuminating the shadows and helping you to see clearly.

Blow the candle out, close your eyes and remember what you saw and thought about. Can you keep that image of comfort in your mind?

Concluding Reflection

The light shines in the darkness and the darkness has not overcome it.
(John 1:5)

The candle

You have been using a candle as a focus for reflection. There are many varieties of lights. The comforting light of a fireside, the clear pathway of a torch beam on a dark night showing the way, the blaze of fireworks in a night sky, the flashing beam of a lighthouse warning of danger.

Bring to mind the person or anxiety you were reflecting about when you were looking at the candle. Which kind of light is needed most?

- A light to show the pathway and help to make a decision as to which path to choose?
- A light to comfort, warm and give reassurance?
- A chance to enjoy celebratory lights and affirm achievements?
- A warning light urging you to steer clear of rocks which could harm?

Draw or write about your choice of light in the space below.

Pebbles in the pool

Have you ever dropped a pebble into a pond and watched the circle of ripples spreading outwards? The effect of the pebble dropping into the water is amazingly wide, reaching further than one might have guessed.

It is the same with the way we choose to behave and with the decisions we make. Each decision or action has a 'knock on' or 'wave' effect on a circle of people nearby and the communities far beyond ourselves.

Sometimes when we are reflecting on the needs of others we can feel overwhelmed by the size of the problems around us. This exercise is to help us to realise the effect of quite small 'pebbles' of love thrown into the 'pool' of our communities.

Sit in a comfortable position and if it helps you, close your eyes, or you may prefer to have a focus of a group of pebbles to look at or simply hold a pebble in your hand.

Think of a positive manner in which you could choose to act for the next hour:

- Helpfully and in the spirit of co-operation?
- Confidently, trusting that you can overcome problems?
- Showing kindness and appreciating the problems of others?
- Being generous and willing to share?

Now imagine yourself into one situation which you will meet during the next hour or during the day:

- Where will you be?
- Who will you meet?

- What decisions will you have to make?
- Imagine yourself behaving in the one particular mood or manner you have chosen – kind, generous, sympathetic etc.

In your imagination watch the effects of your behaviour on the people around you. Now imagine what one of those people will be doing next:

- Have they carried the effects of your behaviour with them?
- Who else is now affected?
- Is it for better or worse?

If possible do the exercise on the Focus Page with a friend.

Concluding Reflection

In stillness we remember all those whose lives are linked to ours and who are affected by our actions or our lack of concern:

The circle of our family and relations
The circle of our friends
The circle of our school community and the students and staff with whom we come into contact
The community of our street, our village, our town
Any places where we meet to work or for recreation

We pray that all our actions may lead to ripples of peace and joy and love which spread into the world. Amen.

Pebbles in the pool

The following diagram shows the ripples on a pool made by the pebble drawn in the centre.

On the pebble in the centre write an action you might take, this could be for good or ill. For example it might be being patient with a younger brother or sister in the morning, or it could be being co-operative to the bus driver on the way to school. In the surrounding circles write down the effects of your action on those nearest to you and then on those further beyond. You might like to do this exercise with a friend and to discuss your thoughts and opinions.

Sixth Prayer Mood

TRUSTING

Christians are people who have decided to put their faith in God and to trust the person of Jesus Christ as the basis for their lives. Perhaps the modern word for people who live by faith should be 'risk takers', for people of faith risk that whatever they are trusting as the basis for their lives is true.

This is not always easy for there are times when God seems very far away and doubts attack peace of mind. Perhaps Jesus himself experienced this in the Garden of Gethsemane and on the cross when he called out, 'My God, my God, why have you forsaken me?' Doubting and uncertainty are not the opposite of faith but faith's companions leading the 'risk takers' to deeper understanding of what a life of faith means.

The following exercises look at attitudes of faith and trust and consider their effects in our daily lives. Prayer Focus 21 uses some biblical phrases to help us to recall God's reassurance to his followers and the encouragement to trust in God's loving purposes for us. Prayer Focus 22 suggests games to help us to trust others and to be discerning as to whom we trust. Prayer Focus 23 explores the basis of our trust whilst Prayer Focus 24 looks at where the events and decisions of your life have led you and reflects on whether an attitude of trust and faith has been a hallmark of your life so far.

Let go and let God

Sometimes we can be tempted to think that everything depends on us rather than trusting God. This can make our bodies feel anxious and tense.

The following exercises are designed to help you to recognise the difference between your body when it is feeling tense and when it is relaxed, and to remember the promises of God's ever-present help by bringing to mind simple phrases from the Bible.

Find a comfortable chair where you can sit with your back and neck easily supported and both feet placed on the ground. If possible place the chair where you have a distant view or, if this is not available, allow your eyes to rest in mid-distance without focusing them on anything specific.

Focus attention on each part of your body in turn, firstly tightening the muscles as hard as you can and holding the tension for a few seconds, then slowly releasing the tension until the muscle feels relaxed and loose.

Focus your attention on one group of muscles at a time:

- your toes
- the calves of your legs
- your thighs
- your bottom
- your stomach
- your hands
- your neck and shoulders
- your face.

Now attend to your breathing. Notice the speed and depth of each breath. Count slowly as you breathe in, and then out. Concentrate on these breaths for five complete 'in and outs'.

Now read the passages on the Focus Page and choose one or part of one as a focus for your prayer. Read it several times so that you know it and do not have to look back at the book. When you have chosen your phrase, put the book aside and return to your relaxed position.

Focus yourself on your breathing and when you feel ready repeat the phrase to yourself with each breath in and out.

The sentences are divided into two parts by asterisks so that there is one phrase for the drawing in of a breath and another for the release.

Let go and let God

*My help comes from the Lord**
who made heaven and earth.
Psalm 121:2

*I am with you always**
to the end of time.
Matthew 28:20
(New English Bible)

Come unto me all you that are weary
*and are carrying heavy burdens,**
and I will give you rest.
Matthew 11:28

*Be still**
and know that I am God.
Psalm 46:10

*Surely God is my salvation.**
I will trust and not be afraid.
Isaiah 12:2

*For I, the Lord your God,**
hold your right hand;
it is I who say to you,
'Do not fear, I will help you.'*
Isaiah 41:13

*But those who wait for the Lord**
shall renew their strength,
*they shall mount up with wings**
*like eagles,**
they shall run and not be weary,*
they shall walk and not faint.*
Isaiah 40:31

*Do not let your hearts be troubled.**
Believe in God, believe also in me.
John 14:1

*I will not leave you orphaned;**
I am coming to you.
John 14:18

*Be strong and bold;**
*have no fear or dread of them,**
because it is the Lord your God
*who goes with you;**
he will not fail you or forsake you.*
Deuteronomy 31:6

*Wait for the Lord;**
be strong and let your heart take courage.
Psalm 27:14

A trust game

Learning to trust others can be difficult, especially if we have been hurt or our experiences in life have made us fearful of the motives of others. The following games are designed to help us to be discerning in whom we trust and to restore our trust in each other.

True or false

A human maze is formed by holding hands. It can be varied by some people sitting, some standing, some close to each other and some with only ends of fingers touching. One person is blindfolded and chooses a partner to be their 'eyes'. The partner of the blindfolded person gives verbal directions through the maze, e.g. one step forward, two steps to the right, beware low obstacle, etc. The game is then repeated with a different maze formation and two different partners for the blindfolded person. This time one of the partners gives accurate directions to lead the person through the maze and the other gives false directions. The blindfolded person has to learn which voice to trust and choose their steps accordingly.

Trust balance

Two people stand facing each other with feet slightly apart and fingertips just touching. It helps if the partners are roughly the same height and build. They then lean forward with their bodies at a slight angle so that the palms of their hands meet and gradually move backwards and forwards, each bending the elbows and taking the weight of each other alternately. They can then repeat the exercise stepping a little further away from each other.

(Adapted from *Let's Play Together* by Milder Masheder. Green Print.)

A trust game

True or false?

Trust balance

What do you trust in?

Choosing for ourselves is one of the joys and one of the problems of becoming adult. One of those choices is what we will put our faith in and trust our life to. Very few people live a life without faith, but the centres of their faith are varied. Some put their faith in having power and influence, some in making money, some in success, some in feeling that everyone likes them. Understanding where you feel your faith lies helps you to realise what influences the decisions you make.

Where do you think you put your trust and faith?

Read through the following statements carefully. Each one contains the seeds of trust in an aspect of our lives and relationships, e.g. wealth, power, popularity. Mark each sentence according to how strongly you agree or disagree, using the following:

✓✓ completely agree

✓ agree

✗ disagree

✗✗ completely disagree.

- I must succeed at everything I do.
- To feel happy in life I must make a lot of money.
- I like to feel that my life helps other people in some way.
- Feeling happy all the time is really essential to me.

- I believe pain or difficulty would ruin my life.
- I want other people to like me at all times.
- I must make my life as perfect as possible.
- I want other people to think I am strong.
- As long as I keep myself to myself I shall be safe.

Read through your answers carefully. On the Focus Page opposite, circle the cartoon(s) which illustrate(s) the sentences you marked ✓ or ✓✓.

Look at each sentence in turn and preferably with a friend ask yourself the following questions:

- Is the sentence a realistic possibility for your life?
- What do you fear about not fulfilling the hopes of each sentence?
- Supposing you were unsuccessful? Poor? Ill?
- Can you face those fears?
- What do the answers reveal about your life?
- What do the answers reveal about where you put your trust?
- Do you feel that is what you want to be the basis of your life?

What do you trust in?

A life map

We often continue our lives day by day without any recollection or consideration of an overall pattern or purpose. This exercise is designed to help us reflect on our life journey, call to mind the influences and events for good or ill, and consider what we have used as a basis for our trust.

Find a reasonably large piece of blank paper or you could use the space on the Focus Page. You may like to photocopy and enlarge the Focus Page to give more scope for detail. Find some felt-tipped pens and take yourself to a place where you can be alone and uninterrupted.

Starting with your birth draw your 'Life map' up to the present moment. It may take several sessions to complete this. You can use words, symbols, pictures or patterns to help describe your life. Consider:

- When and where were you born?

- Who was in your family at that time and where did they live?

- What was your place in the family? First grandchild? Second son?

- Who are the people in your map?

- What are the important events? (These could be family events, local events you remember or national events which are significant to you. You may like to mark happy events in one colour and sad events in another colour.)

- Where have you had to make important decisions?

- What or who has influenced you in your journey?

- Are there parts of your life which seemed fun?

- Are there parts which were difficult?

Concluding Reflection

Look carefully at your map:

- What do you learn from it?

- Can you see any pattern?

- At which points did you feel you were going in the right direction?

- Were there places where you felt lost?

- Can you reflect on who or what guided or influenced you when you made decisions?

- What do you want to make the basis for your decisions in the future?

- What feels the right direction for your life at the present moment?

- Do you want to share any of your discoveries with anyone?

- Who will you choose to speak with? When? Where?

A life map

Seventh Prayer Mood

IMAGINATIVE CONTEMPLATION

When we are familiar with a story from the Bible it is easy to lose the real sense of what the story is about and to be unaware of its original impact.

The aim of this prayer mood is to enter imaginatively into the story and to consider how different people in the story might be feeling. To 'consider' has several layers of meaning:

- to turn over in one's mind
- to observe carefully
- remember and recall
- to empathise or be aware of another's need.

This imaginative contemplation may provide an opportunity for reflection and might give you insight into your own life.

For the following four exercises you will need a Bible. It would be helpful to choose a version with which you feel comfortable and it might help your reflections to look at some pictures of the Holy Land so that you can imagine the setting of the story. It would also help to find out something about life at the time of Jesus.

This exercise can be done alone or in groups. It is sometimes helpful to share the insights different people have from the exercise.

For each of the stories the procedure is the same:

1 Reading and familiarisation

- Read the story through carefully as many times as you need, to become thoroughly familiar with the events and the people in the story.

- Set the scene: is the story set in a house or outside? Is it by a lake or a mountain or on a dusty road. Allow all your senses of sight, hearing, smell, touch and taste to absorb the story. Experience the sun, dust, soothing ointment, touch of Jesus or whatever strikes you as you read.

- Think about the events: who are the characters? What is the sequence of events? What actually happens?

- Consider the feelings of the characters in the story. Are they afraid, sad, angry, embarrassed, joyful? Do their moods change and if so, how?

2 Visualising

Choose one of the characters and imagine that you are this character whilst you read the story again or tell it to yourself. If you are working in a group or with a partner, you may like to take turns in reading the story to each other.

3 Reflecting on the story

Perhaps with your eyes closed let the story speak to you and consider what important insights you have discovered through the reading. You may like to use the questions provided to help you.

4 Returning to the present

When you have finished the exercise leave the scene of the story, and bringing with you what you have learned, return to the present. You may use the same story several times becoming a different character each time.

The lost son

1 Read the story of the lost son in Luke 15:11-32.

- Set the scene: As you are reading imagine the scene – it may help your imagination to find a book which gives an idea of the landscape, the methods of farming at that time, the methods of travel, the social customs.

    Think carefully about the phrases: 'Into a far country'; what would that mean? A long journey by foot? By donkey or camel? Would there be any contact? Certainly no telephones! What chance was there of a message or letter?

    'His elder son was in the field'; what would he be farming? What tools would he have? Would the climate present difficulties? It may take a complete prayer time simply to 'set the scene' of the story.

- Think about the events: Who are the characters in the story? Where does the story take place? Does the story unfold in different places? You may need to read it several times until the details are clearly in your mind. What are the feelings?

- Consider the feelings: Try to identify the feelings of all the characters. Be aware of the moods of the story and the changing feelings of the characters?

2 Visualising: Choose to be one of the characters in the story: the father, the elder son, the younger son, one of the servants. Read the story through twice whilst imagining yourself as that character. Be aware of how you are feeling, of the words spoken to you; be aware of changes in your feeling or attitudes. What do you discover about the feelings of the character you have chosen? How do they feel at the beginning of the story? In the middle of the story? At the end of the story?

3 Reflecting on the story: Put the Bible aside and reflect on your discoveries. Which part of the story spoke to you most? Which event was most vivid? Were there any words or phrases which seemed especially important to you? Does what you discover give you insight or understanding of any of your relationships? Does what you discover alter your understanding of your relationship with God?

4 Leave the scene of the story and, bringing with you what you have learned, return to the present.

The woman who washed Jesus' feet

1 Read the story of the woman who washed Jesus' feet in Luke 7:36-50.

- Set the scene: Who are the characters? Jesus, Simon the Pharisee, the 'woman of the city'. Do you imagine other guests or disciples were there?

  Look at verse 29: 'those who were at table with him'. Who might these people have been? What was a Pharisee? Would this have been the house of a rich or poor man? Was a Pharisee an influential and powerful person? How did people eat at the time of Jesus? When Jesus 'sat at table' how do you visualise this?

  What do you know about the practice of washing the feet of visitors which happened in hot countries where they may have travelled on dusty roads?

  How do you imagine the 'woman of the city'. Was she a vagrant? A prostitute? Someone who was well-to-do but considered by the Pharisees to have sinned?

- Think about the events: The preparations for the meal and the arrival of the guests and Jesus' arrival. The unexpected arrival of the woman with the flask of ointment. The woman crying and washing Jesus' feet with her tears. The woman drying Jesus' feet with her hair and anointing them with ointment. The reactions of Jesus and the Pharisee. The effect of Jesus' words on the Pharisee and the woman.

- Consider the feelings of the people in the story: Think of their feelings before the event, as the event happened and unfolded, at the end of Jesus' words to Simon and to the woman. Be aware of the feelings. Are they of excitement? Anticipation? Fear? Annoyance? Humiliation? Anger? Relief? Amazement? Joy? Release?

2 Visualising: Choose and imagine yourself as one of the characters in the story, such as Jesus, the Pharisee Simon, the woman, one of the guests. Now read the story again or tell it to yourself imagining yourself to be that character. Be conscious of your feelings as the tale unfolds. Watch the faces of the people around you and their reactions. Listen to what Jesus and Simon say and note your own feelings and the reactions of the other people.

3 Reflect on what you have discovered. Which feelings or events were particularly vivid for you? Did any event or words stand out for you? Do you have further insight into the person of Jesus? Do you understand more about Jesus' perception of people? Do you have any insights into the ways you or others behave?

4 Leave the scene of the story and, bringing with you what you have learned, return to the present.

The man who wanted to see Jesus

1 Read the story of Zacchaeus the chief tax collector in Luke 19:1-10.

- Set the scene: Who are the characters? Zacchaeus, Jesus, the crowd. Who was Zacchaeus?

  Look at verses 2 and 3. Do you suppose being a 'chief' tax collector meant that he was a person of some power? Who was he collecting taxes for? Do you think he was popular? If he was rich do you think he would have been wearing fine clothes? Imagine running ahead or climbing a tree in splendid clothes.

  Look at verse 3: Zacchaeus is described as being 'small of stature'. How do you think being small affected his self-image? Verse 3 also says 'he sought to see who Jesus was'. What do you imagine Zacchaeus wanted from Jesus? Do you know what a sycamore tree looks like?

- Think about the events: Zacchaeus trying to find a place where he could see Jesus, the crowds wanting to be near Jesus, Zacchaeus having the idea of where he could best see.

- Consider the feelings in the story: Anxiety? Surprise? Joy? Annoyance? Resentment? Embarrassment? Relief? Hope? Celebration? What do you

think the crowd thought of Zacchaeus? How do you imagine Zacchaeus felt when Jesus stopped under the tree? How does Jesus' request to stay with Zacchaeus affect the crowd? What is the response of Zacchaeus to Jesus' request? Be aware of the feelings of Jesus and Zacchaeus.

2 Visualising: Choose and imagine yourself as one of the characters in the story: Zacchaeus, Jesus, someone in the crowd. Now read the story through again or tell it to yourself imagining yourself to be that character. Note your feelings. Be aware of the people around you, the expressions on their faces and what they say.

3 Reflect on the story: Which part is most vivid for you? Which events in the story stood out for you? Were any words particularly important for you? Were there any surprises for you when you were in your character? Did your experience tell you something about the character, yourself, or the person of Jesus which you had not noticed before?

4 Leave the scene of the story and, bringing with you what you have learned, return to the present.

Jesus meets a rich man

1 Read the story of the conversation between Jesus and the rich young man in Mark 10:17-27.

- Set the scene: Jesus, the young man, the disciples; were there other people listening? How do you visualise the man?

  Look at verse 17; 'he ran up and knelt' before Jesus. Did he just manage to catch Jesus before he left that place? What does his kneeling suggest about the way he regarded Jesus? The man addresses Jesus as 'Good Teacher'. What do you think he meant?

- Think about the events: Jesus about to leave, the way Jesus looked at the man, the reactions of the man and the bystanders.

- Consider the feelings of the people involved. Anticipation? Love? Hope? Concern? Disappointment? Sorrow? Amazement? Confusion?

2 Visualising: Choose and imagine yourself as one of the people in the story: Jesus, the rich man, one of the disciples or the crowd. Be aware of the events and the feelings as you retell the story to yourself. Listen carefully to the words as they are spoken. Be aware of your own reactions and the reactions of others. How do you feel as you hear Jesus' command to the man: 'Go sell what you have and give to the poor'? How do you feel as the man 'went away sorrowful'?

3 Reflect on the story as you read it as your character. What did you notice particularly? Which words spoke most forcefully to you? What was your overriding emotion? Did the story give you insights into your own life and the way you make decisions?

4 Leave the scene of the story and, bringing with you what you have learned, return to the present.